Soldiers of the French and Indian War

Diane Smolinski

Series Consultant:
Lieutenant Colonel G.A. LoFaro

Heinemann Library
Chicago, Illinois

© 2003 Reed Educational & Professional Publishing
Published by Heinemann Library,
an imprint of Reed Educational & Professional
Publishing, Chicago, Illinois

Customer Service 888-454-2279

Visit our website at www.heinemannlibrary.com

Designed by Herman Adler Design
Photo research by Julie Laffin
Printed and bound in the United States by Lake Book
Manufacturing, Inc.

07 06 05 04 03
10 9 8 7 6 5 4 3 2 1

Library of Congress Cataloging-in-Publication Data
Smolinski, Diane, 1950-
  Soldiers of the French and Indian War / Diane
Smolinski.
      p. cm. -- (Americans at war. The French and
Indian War)
Includes bibliographical references and index.
  ISBN 1-4034-0172-1
  1. United States--History--French and Indian War,
1755-1763--Juvenile literature. 2. United States--Armed
Forces--History--French and Indian War, 1755-1763--
Juvenile literature. 3. Soldiers--United
States--History--18th century--Juvenile literature. [1.
United States--History--French and Indian War, 1755-
1763.] I. Title.
  E199 .S665 2002
  973.2'6--dc21
                                        2002005082

Acknowledgments
The author and publishers are grateful to the following
for permission to reproduce copyright material:
Contents page, pp. 8, 11B, 17R, 19, 21B, 23B, Peter
Newark's Military Pictures; pp. 5, 29 William L.
Clements Library, University of Michigan, Ann Arbor;
pp. 6, 9, 17L, 18, North Wind Picture Archives; p. 7
Rich Nardi/American Powderhorns; pp. 10, 11T, 14, 20,
21T, 22, 25L, 27 Mary Evans Picture Library; p. 12
The Company of Military Historians from the book,
*Military Uniforms in America: The Era of the American
Revolution 1755-1795*, plate #378; p.13 Joseph Sohm/
ChromoSohm, Inc./Corbis; pp. 15, 23T, 24 The Granger
Collection, New York; p. 16 Heinemann Library; p. 25R
Portrait of an Unidentified French Admiral, late 18th Century,
#M985.218 Notman Photographic Archives, McCord
Museum of Canadian History, Montreal; p. 26 Wolfgang
Kaehler/Corbis; p. 28 Archivo Iconografico, S.A./Corbis.

Cover photographs: (main) Bettmann/Corbis, (border,
T-B) Corbis, Sue Emerson/Heinemann Library.

About the Author
Diane Smolinski is the author of two previous series of
books on the Revolutionary and Civil Wars. She earned
degrees in education from Duquesne and Slippery Rock
Universities and taught in public schools for 28 years.
Diane now writes for teachers, helping them to use
nonfiction books in their classrooms. She currently
lives in Florida with her husband, Henry, and their
cat, Pepper.

Special thanks to Gary Barr for offering comments from
a teacher's perspective.

About the Consultant
G.A. LoFaro is a lieutenant colonel in the U.S. Army
currently stationed at Fort McPherson, Georgia. After
graduating from West Point, he was commissioned in
the infantry. He has served in a variety of positions in
the 82nd Airborne Division, the Ranger Training
Brigade, and Second Infantry Division in Korea. He has
a Masters Degree in U.S. History from the University of
Michigan and is completing his Ph.D in U.S. History at
the State University of New York at Stony Brook. He has
also served six years on the West Point faculty where he
taught military history to cadets.

On the cover: This illustration shows Generals Wolfe and Montcalm at the Battle of Quebec, September 1759.
On the contents page: French General Montcalm celebrates his victory over British and colonial troops after the Battle of Fort
Carillon (Ticonderoga) in 1758.

Note to the Reader
The terms North American Indian, Indian, Indian Nation, or the specific tribe names are used here instead of Native American.
These terms are historically accurate for the time period covered in this book.

Some words are shown in bold, **like this.**
You can find out what they mean by looking in the glossary.

Contents

Introduction

During the 1700s, France and Great Britain competed for land and trade opportunities on the continent of North America east of the Mississippi River. Britain and France also fought against each other for power on the continent of Europe. This European conflict was called the Seven Years' War. The struggle for power in North America between these two nations was part of this European War. It was called the French and Indian War.

Even though the British did not officially declare war on France in North America until May of 1756, fighting involving the French, the Indians, and the British became more and more regular by 1753.

The British controlled most of the land along the eastern coastline that was considered the thirteen North American **colonies.** *The land that France controlled was to the west in the Great Lakes area in what is today part of Canada. This land was called New France. The Spanish arrived in the late 1400s and claimed territories along the southern and western parts of North America.*

KEY
French claim
British claim
Spanish claim
French and British claim
Spanish and British claim

Organizing Armies

As the fighting between the British and French became more intense, both countries needed to increase the size of their armies in North America. Most of their **regular military force** was fighting and protecting territories in other parts of the world at this time. As each country realized a need to protect their North American territories and the **economic resources** within them, each country sent additional regular army troops from their homeland to North America.

More Troops are Needed

Even though many British regulars arrived, more soldiers were needed. They **recruited** American colonists to serve in the British Army, and also requested that the individual colonies send their **militia** to help. France also sent regular army soldiers to Canada to fight in the war. Like the British, the French needed the help of their colonists and militia as well.

In addition, the French were able to recruit large numbers of Indians to help them battle the British. Some Indians also fought on the side of the British, but in much smaller numbers.

Members of the British Army came to the colonies in search of volunteers. Here, a British officer is measuring a colonist. The colonist stands on his tiptoes in order to pass the test and be allowed to fight in the war.

Most colonies required all males between the ages of 16 and 60 to serve in the militia. They were supposed to meet during the year and stay ready to help defend the community.

Colonial Militia

During the 1700s, Great Britain, France, and Spain claimed and ruled different parts of North America. Each of these countries was responsible for protecting their **colonies.**

The North American colonies of Great Britain did not have a professional **regular** army, but each of these colonies had its own **militia.** During the French and Indian War, the militia helped to defend the boundaries of its own colony and occasionally joined **forces** with other colonial militia to help battle the French and Indian forces.

Each of the colonial governments chose their high-ranking militia officers. These officers often held important positions in their communities.

Frontier Dispatch

- Militia officers of a lesser rank were selected by the militia soldiers.

- The Royal Governor or the colonial assembly of each colony decided when to call the militia into action.

The Militia of the Massachusetts Colony

This is an example of how the militia of the colony of Massachusetts was organized in 1756.

The governor of the colony called for volunteers. In 1756, a sign-up bonus, or bounty, was offered. If a volunteer brought his own gun, he was paid an additional bounty. Men were **drafted** from the community if not enough volunteered. Men were usually required to sign up for the length of the **campaign,** but no longer than one year.

The Massachusetts colony provided their militia volunteers with:

- a **musket**—a gun (if a volunteer did not have his own);
- a powder horn—a funnel-shaped storage container for gunpowder;
- a bullet pouch—a small, pocket-sized bag that held musket balls;
- a blanket;
- a knapsack—a bag, similar to a backpack, for carrying personal items; and
- a canteen—a container for drinking water.

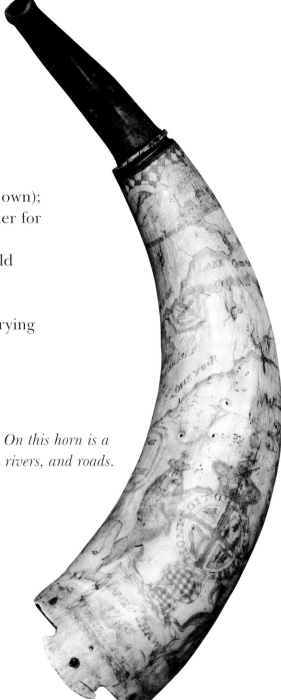

Militia volunteers would have had powder horns like this. On this horn is a map of the Ohio River Territory complete with forts, lakes, rivers, and roads.

Infantry

Most soldiers in both the British and French armies served in the infantry.

Professional Soldiers

Regular infantry soldiers from France and Great Britain were trained to march in straight, neat **columns** from battle to battle. They stood shoulder-to-shoulder in lines to load and fire their weapons and then charge with their **bayonets.** This type of fighting did prove valuable in the French and Indian War at times, however the thickly forested wilderness lands of North America often made this style of warfare ineffective.

The North American Indians used the cover of the forest to surprise and attack their enemy. Both the French and the British needed to learn to fight in this way and to protect themselves against this style of attack.

Frontier Dispatch

Firing and Charging in Ranks

Standing shoulder-to-shoulder, soldiers formed three rows, one behind the other, facing the enemy. On command, each row took turns firing at the approaching enemy. As soon as they fired, they quickly reloaded their **musket** so that they would be ready when it was again their turn to fire. By firing together as a row, it made up for the inaccuracy of the musket. After firing several **volleys,** they would charge with their bayonets.

The British Army in North America formed a unit called "Rogers Rangers." Robert Rogers led and trained his men to attack enemies much like the Indians. They used the trees as cover and wore green uniforms to blend in with the color of the forest, similar to what these Indians are doing.

Moving artillery through the wilderness was difficult. The Army needed to bring food and water for the horses that pulled the cannons. Rivers or steep hills often forced the Army to stop and look for another route to take.

In 1754, many roads were poor or nonexistent in the wilderness areas. This made it difficult for soldiers to march and for horses to pull **artillery** and equipment wagons. Wagons carried items such as ammunition, food for the soldiers, tents, and officers' personal items. Soldiers often had to cut trees and build roads to pass through this wilderness.

Equipment

Soldiers in both the French and British regular armies were supplied with uniforms, weapons, boots, blankets, eating utensils, canteens, **cartridge** boxes, and knapsacks.

Colonial militiamen often had to provide their own clothing, but may have been given some other supplies. Each colony had different rules about issuing supplies.

Frontier Dispatch

- In some areas, such as in the Niagara Region, many lakes and rivers made it easy for infantrymen to travel by boat. Boats could move men and equipment more quickly and efficiently than by marching.

- Drummers marched with each company. They provided a beat for marching soldiers, and provided a way to send a commanding officer's orders to the men.

Weapons

The long-barreled **musket** was the main weapon of the French and British **infantryman** and the **colonial militiaman.** This gun fired a small, round lead ball, called a musket ball. The soldier usually bit open a **cartridge,** poured a small amount of gunpowder into a pan and the rest down the barrel of the gun. He then pushed the musket ball and the paper cartridge into the barrel with a wood or iron rod. When the soldier pulled the trigger, a spark lit the gunpowder and caused the musket to fire. A **bayonet** could be attached to the end of the barrel for hand-to-hand combat. It also provided a means by which infantrymen could defend themselves against enemy **cavalry.**

Even though the musket was the most widely used weapon during the French and Indian War, it was not very accurate. It often did not fire when the gunpowder got wet, and was slow to reload.

*An infantry soldier could fire a musket about two times a minute. The smoke and confusion during battle made it difficult to reload, giving the well-trained **regular** soldier an advantage over the inexperienced colonial militiaman.*

Frontier Dispatch

- The most common model of musket used by the British infantry was the Long Land Musket, also called the "Brown Bess." It shot a round lead ball about ¾ inch (2 cm) in diameter, had a barrel that was 42 inches (107 cm) long, and a bayonet that was about 14 inches (36 cm) long.

- The French musket was similar, except it used a smaller musket ball.

French Infantry Uniforms

The French infantryman was issued a dress uniform that included:

- a grey-white wool coat with blue cuffs;
- grey-white knee breeches—trousers or pants that came to the knee;
- white gaiters—a covering over the shoe and lower leg; and
- a black tri-cornered hat—a hat with the edge turned up to form three sides and three corners.

British Infantry Uniforms

The British infantryman of the regular army was issued a standard uniform that included:

- a red wool coat;
- a waistcoat—vest;
- a white shirt;
- red wool breeches—trousers or pants that came to the knee;
- black, brown, or gray gaiters—a covering over the shoe and lower leg;
- black leather shoes;
- a black tri-cornered hat—a hat with the edge turned up to form three sides and three corners; and
- a crossbelt with cartridge box—small container that held gunpowder and musket balls.

Frontier Dispatch

When the **regiments** arrived in North America, some adopted uniforms that better suited the climate and conditions. For example, the 60th Regiment of Foot of the British Army wore hunting shirts and Indian leggings for a short time.

Both French and British infantrymen were issued similar uniforms and equipment. The British were usually easy to spot due to their red coats.

Artillery

Men in both armies were trained to fire and maintain cannons called artillery. Soldiers who manned the cannons were called gunners. Moving cannons in North America at this time was difficult. The land was hilly and heavily forested, with few wide or well-developed roads.

Getting Ready to Fire

Loading and firing the cannons was slow. The barrel had to be cleaned after each firing. A long rod with a **swab** at one end cleared the barrel of debris. Then, gunpowder and packing, such as straw or cloth, was pushed into the barrel followed by a cannon ball. The gunpowder was lit through a hole at the back of the cannon, causing it to fire.

A trained group of soldiers could fire a cannon about once every four minutes.

Frontier Dispatch

One way that a cannon was named was by the weight of the shell. Shells could weigh 3, 6, 9, 12, or 24 pounds (1, 3, 4, 5, or 11 kilograms).

These garrison cannons are at Fort Carillon, also known as Fort Ticonderoga. Fort Carillon was located just north of Lake George and thus needed the protection of these large cannons on many occasions.

Field Artillery

Field cannons moved with the **infantry** as the foot soldiers attacked an enemy position. A cannon could be attached to a two-wheeled wooden frame for horses or oxen to pull to the site of the battle. Horse-drawn wagons carried the ammunition. Artillery fire could destroy attacking troops or protect troops that were defending a fixed position.

Garrison and Siege Artillery

Garrison and siege artillery were larger types of cannons. They were not intended to be moved. Garrison, or fortress, cannons were positioned at a fort to protect it from an attacking army or to control important waterways.

Siege cannons were used against an enemy that was trapped or surrounded. They were big and heavy and could not be moved easily. These cannons fired larger-sized cannonballs that traveled longer distances than field artillery. Siege cannons were used to attack forts and buildings.

Cavalry

Cavalry soldiers rode horses. Cavalry units were small in number compared to **infantry** units. They rode ahead of foot soldiers, or infantry, and gathered information about the opposing army. They also rode on the ends of the infantry lines on the battlefield and protected **columns** of soldiers as they marched from and into battle.

The **saber** was the most effective weapon of the cavalry rider, but they also carried pistols and **carbines.** Cavalry troops had unique uniforms. They may have worn heavy boots to protect their legs from the high undergrowth of the wilderness, as well as a helmet for protection.

Both the French and British had cavalry units called dragoons. Dragoons were infantrymen who rode horses.

Thick forests and steep hills made it difficult for the cavalry to participate in many battles during the French and Indian War.

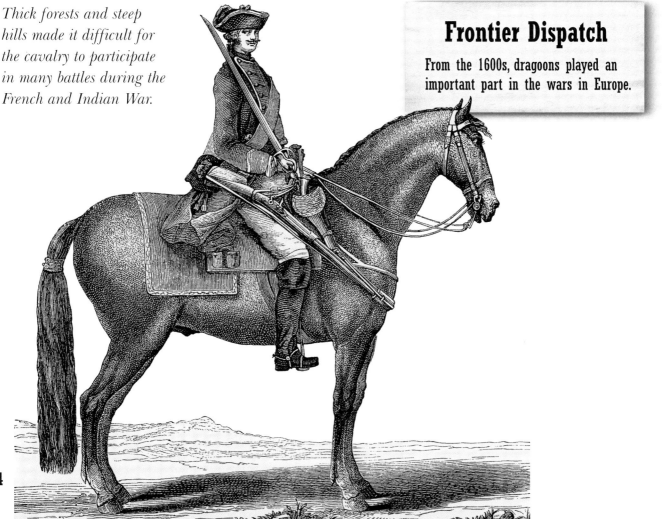

Frontier Dispatch

From the 1600s, dragoons played an important part in the wars in Europe.

Forts

Even before the war started, settlers in frontier lands built forts for protection from Indian attacks. Forts built by the military **forces** of France and England were usually designed to protect important places such as cities, rivers, **harbors,** and the borders of countries.

Star Forts

Some of the first forts built in North America resembled the shape of a star. They were usually made of stone and soil and often protected cities or harbors.

Stockade Forts

Forts built in the frontier territories were primarily stockade forts. The walls were made of logs placed upright in the ground. They were rectangular in shape and more common than star forts because they were easier and quicker to build.

During the French and Indian War, many battles were fought for the control of forts.

Fort Oswego (left) in New York is an example of a star fort, while Fort Necessity (right) in Pennsylvania is a stockade fort.

Frontier Dispatch

Wooden blockhouses were sometimes built on each corner of a stockade fort. A blockhouse was a building that protected soldiers while they were shooting at the attacking enemy. It had small, cutout holes in the walls to shoot weapons through.

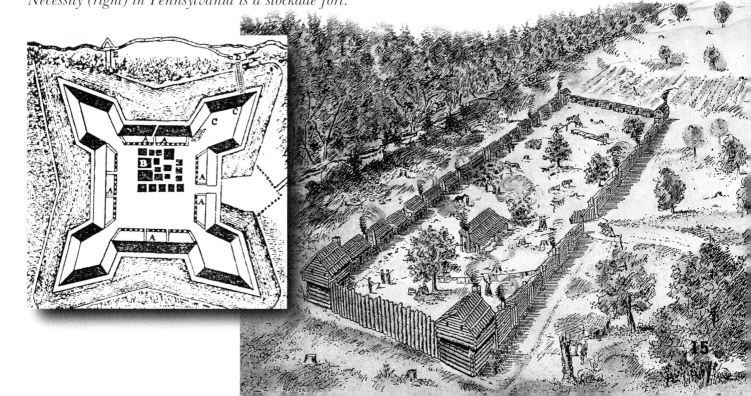

British Army Leaders

Officers from both France and England were chosen in several ways. Some men from wealthy families paid to get positions as officers. They joined the military to gain power in the government and for personal fame. Other men who were not wealthy had to earn their positions based on their experience in the military. Professional officers were well trained and disciplined.

Frontier Dispatch

The **commanders in chief** of the British **forces** from 1755 to the end of the French and Indian War were Braddock, Shirley, Webb, Abercromby, Loudoun, and Amherst.

British Army Leaders

Many British generals were sent to lead British and **colonial** troops in North America throughout the war. These officers brought experience to the battlefields.

In some British families, serving in the military was a tradition.
Some families could trace their military service back many generations.

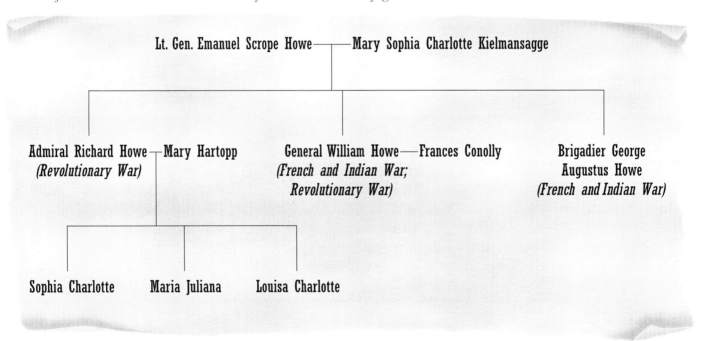

Lt. Gen. Emanuel Scrope Howe — Mary Sophia Charlotte Kielmansagge

Admiral Richard Howe — Mary Hartopp
(Revolutionary War)

General William Howe — Frances Conolly
(French and Indian War;
Revolutionary War)

Brigadier George
Augustus Howe
(French and Indian War)

Sophia Charlotte   Maria Juliana   Louisa Charlotte

The site where Fort Duquesne sat is today part of the present-day city of Pittsburgh, Pennsylvania.

Frontier Dispatch

- George Washington was one of General Braddock's aides.

- As they retreated from Fort Duquesne, Braddock's men buried him on July 14, 1755 on the path back to Fort Cumberland, Virginia. All the men marched over his grave to camouflage the grave site. They did not want any Indians to find him and disturb his grave.

General Edward Braddock
1695–1755

Born in Perthshire, Scotland in 1695, Edward Braddock joined the British Army in 1710 when he was only fifteen years old.

During the War

In 1755, Braddock arrived in the North American colony of Virginia and became commander in chief of the British forces in North America. His first mission was to attack Fort Duquesne. This French fort was in the Ohio River Territory, the area where the Allegheny and Monongahela Rivers meet to form the Ohio River. As his troops marched toward Fort Duquesne, they were attacked and defeated by a group of French, Canadians, and Indians. Braddock was wounded during the battle and died four days later on July 13, 1755.

General Edward Braddock

General William Shirley
1694–1771

William Shirley was born in Preston, England, in 1694. He became a lawyer and moved to Boston, Massachusetts, in 1731. Ten years later he became the Royal Governor of Massachusetts.

During the War

Shirley was appointed the **commander in chief** of British **forces** in North America in 1755, after the death of General Edward Braddock. During the French and Indian War, Shirley failed to defeat the French in the New York **colony** area and was recalled to England.

After the War

Shirley remained in England until 1761, when he was appointed the governor of the **Bahamas.** He served as the governor of the Bahamas for eight years and then retired to the Massachusetts colony, where he died in 1771.

Shirley was well-liked and a successful governor of the colony of Massachusetts, but he was not able to achieve this same success as a military leader.

Frontier Dispatch

In 1755, William Shirley, the new commander in chief of the British forces, made a plan to capture Nova Scotia, Fort Niagara, and Lake George. Shirley would lead the attack on Fort Niagara. He assigned Colonel William Johnson to attack at Lake George, and Colonel Monckton would go to Nova Scotia.

General Jeffery Amherst
1717–1797

Jeffery Amherst was born in Sevenoaks, England, in 1717. At age fourteen, he joined the British Army. While fighting in wars in Europe, he gained much experience and became a capable leader.

During the War

When he was only 40 years old, Jeffery Amherst was chosen to succeed Lord Loudoun as commander in chief of British forces in North America. Under his leadership, the British captured Fort Louisbourg in Nova Scotia, and defeated the French at the city of Montreal in Canada. He remained in command of the British Army in North America until the end of the war in 1763.

After the War

Amherst returned to England in 1763 and continued to serve in the British Army. He died in 1797.

Both the town of Amherst, Massachusetts and Amherst College are named after General Jeffery Amherst.

Frontier Dispatch

Amherst is famous for his leadership in the capture of Fort Louisbourg. Louisbourg guarded the entrance to the St. Lawrence River. The fall of Fort Louisbourg allowed the British **fleet** to sail down the St. Lawrence and attack the heart of the French colonies of Canada at Quebec and Montreal.

French Army Leaders

Most French regular army leaders were in Europe fighting the Seven Years' War. French army officers were sent to North America once it became apparent that their experience was needed.

Baron Ludwig August Dieskau
1701–1767

In 1755, the French general August Dieskau was sent to take command of French troops in North America. Soon after he arrived, he led French **forces** and their Indian **allies** in an attack against British and **colonial** forces at Lake George (Lac St. Sacrement) in New York. The British and colonial troops defeated the French forces. While recovering from wounds he received from this battle, Dieskau wrote a letter to the French Minister of War, Count d'Argenson, about the battle:

14th September, 1755

As I was near the enemy's camp, … I marched forward with 200 Regulars to capture it, expecting that the Canadians would not abandon me, and that the Indians would perhaps return; but in vain. The Regulars received the whole of the enemy's fire…I was knocked down by three shots…, I know not at present what will be my fate; from Monsieur Johnson, the General of the English army, I am receiving all the attention possible to be expected from a brave man, full of honor and feeling…

Your most humble and Most obedient servant,

Baron de Dieskau

(from pp. 317–318, New York Colonial Documents)

Dieskau was captured at the Battle of Lake George in 1755 and held prisoner. After his recovery, he was transported to England and later released to France where he died in 1767.

Louis Joseph Marquis de Montcalm
1712–1759

Montcalm was born into a wealthy military family. He studied Latin, Greek, and history and was a good student. Montcalm went to school until he was fifteen years old and then joined the French Army, serving in his father's **regiment.** During this time in France, a successful military career would mean success in social and business circles. After two years, his father paid to have him appointed to the rank of captain.

Louis Joseph Marquis de Montcalm

During the War

In 1756, Montcalm was sent to replace Dieskau as the **commander in chief** of French forces in Canada. He won several battles against the British, but in 1759 was defeated at the city of Quebec, Canada, on the **Plains of Abraham,** where he was killed.

Montcalm and his men celebrated a great victory over the British on July 8, 1758 at Fort Carillon. The British troops outnumbered the French, but their poor planning was enough to allow France to win.

Frontier Dispatch

With the defeat of the French at Quebec, the British could organize all of their military strength to capture Montreal. The British came with over 18,000 men, while the French had only 2,100 soldiers well enough to fight. On September 8, 1760, the French surrendered. Smaller **skirmishes** continued for several years at French frontier forts until the end of the war in 1763.

The North American Indians

The French in North America were mainly interested in trading with the North American Indians, while the British wanted to build settlements. The Indians did not want settlers staying on their lands and therefore remained friendlier toward the French.

During the French and Indian War, Indians fought both on the sides of the British and the French, but many more sided with the French. When the British won the war, the Indians were without an **ally.**

Chief Pontiac
c.1720–1769

Pontiac was the chief of a group of Ottawa, Potawatomi, and Ojibwa Indians. Pontiac and his warriors were friendlier toward the French traders than they were toward the British. They would trade furs for supplies such as food, guns, and ammunition. When the French and Indian War began, these Indians sided with the French.

Indians helped the French on many occasions during the French and Indian War. In addition to trading with the French, they also acted as guides and fought beside them.

Indians usually did not attack a fort because they did not have cannons. However, they would surround a fort and wait for the settlers' food and water to run out.

During the War

Pontiac disliked the British because they wanted to take and settle Indian land. Pontiac organized Indian tribes in the Great Lakes area to attack British forts and settlements. He planned to attack Fort Detroit, but his plan was not successful. The British reacted by attacking the Indian camp, but many British were killed or wounded. Other tribes did attack and kill people at other forts in the Great Lakes area and settlements were destroyed.

Little is known about Chief Pontiac's life as a young boy, but as a man he was respected by the Indians for his leadership ability and his accomplishments as a warrior.

After the War

After the war ended, the French were gone, and the British sent troops against the Indians and retook many of the settlements. In 1766, Pontiac agreed to a peace treaty. In 1769, an Indian from another tribe murdered Pontiac.

Navies

Both the British and French depended on their navies to transport troops, carry supplies, and control important waterways. This was a difficult task, as Europe was 3,000 miles (4,828 kilometers) from North America. Furthermore, the waters of the North Atlantic could be icy and rough much of the year, sailors were unfamiliar with the inland waterways of North America, and the technology during this time period was limited.

The British Navy, or Royal Navy as it was also called, was the larger and stronger of the two navies at this time. But the French Navy was also a powerful fighting force. The British were successful, though, in preventing the French from transporting large parts of their army from France to North America.

*The modern **sextant** (right) was invented by John Hadley of England and Thomas Godfrey of Philadelphia, Pennsylvania. The compass (below) was first used by the Chinese in the eighth century C.E.*

Frontier Dispatch

Wooden ships with sails had to battle the fierce winds, high waves, and icy seas. Sailors relied on the stars, compasses, and sextants to guide their ships.

Officers in both the British (left) and French (right) navies wore more formal uniforms than their sailors.

Clothing

The dress of a sailor was much less formal than that of an army soldier at this time. Officers were issued uniforms. The captain could buy clothing for his crew or may require them to bring certain types of clothing. Shoes may not have been worn except in cold weather or when coming ashore.

Some of the common clothing worn by a more experienced sailor at this time included:
- a linen shirt;
- loose fitting pants that came below the knee;
- stockings;
- black shoes;
- a hat;
- a waistcoat—vest;
- a waist- or hip-length jacket; and
- a neckerchief—cloth to wipe sweat or tie back their hair.

Sailors also needed to bring sleeping items such as a hammock, pillows, and a blanket.

Naval Leaders

Admiral de la Motte
1683–1764

De la Motte was born in Rennes, France in 1683 to a wealthy French family. At age sixteen he joined the French Navy, serving on many ships and in many wars for the French.

During the War

In 1757, Admiral de la Motte was placed in charge of a large French **fleet** that sailed from Brest, France to Fort Louisbourg, Nova Scotia. His ships brought troops and supplies to the fort. De la Motte planned to defeat the British fleet that was in the area, but an unexpected, powerful storm arose. With his ships damaged in the storm and many of his sailors ill, Admiral de la Motte decided to return to France rather than fight the British.

De la Motte died at his home in Rennes, France in 1764.

Frontier Dispatch

- When the French and Indian War began, de la Motte was 73 years old.

- Admiral de la Motte's full name was Emmanuel-Auguste de Cahideuc, Comte Dubois de la Motte.

*Fort Louisbourg guarded the entrance to the St. Lawrence River. Whoever controlled Fort Louisbourg, could also control travel in the Great Lakes region and all the **economic resources** found there.*

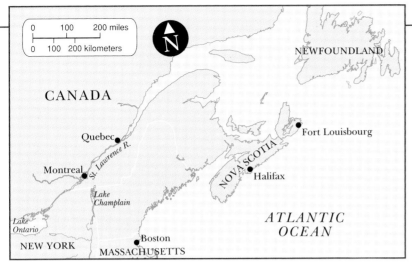

The British could invade Canada by sailing down the St. Lawrence River. They planned to capture Fort Louisbourg, which guarded the entrance to this important waterway. More than 100 ships with over 6,000 British troops sailed from Halifax, Nova Scotia, to Fort Louisbourg.

Admiral Edward Boscawen
1711–1761

Edward Boscawen entered the British Navy when he was fifteen years old. He proved himself a capable leader in naval battles for the British. He was made the captain of the *Dreadnaught*, a 60-gun ship, at the age of 33.

Admiral Edward Boscawen

During the War

Boscawen was placed in charge of a **squadron** of ships that was responsible for **blockading** Fort Louisbourg on the coast of Nova Scotia, keeping French troops and supplies from reaching it. In 1758, Boscawen commanded the fleet that captured Fort Louisbourg.

After this battle, he returned to England and continued to serve in the British Navy. He died of a fever in 1761 at the age of 50.

During the Battle of Fort Louisbourg, British warships fired on French ships until most were destroyed.

The Treaty of Paris

The Treaty of Paris was a peace agreement between Britain, France, and Spain that officially ended the French and Indian War.

Frontier Dispatch

The Treaty of Paris was signed on February 10, 1763 in Paris, France.

The terms of the treaty gave Britain control of nearly all land in North America east of the Mississippi River, including Canada. Spain received New Orleans and the territory west of the Mississippi River, called Louisiana, from a previous treaty with France. They also controlled the island of Cuba. France received two islands in the **West Indies** and two islands off the coast of Newfoundland. They could also fish off the banks of Newfoundland.

After the War

Once the French and Indian War ended, **colonial** settlers traveled west across the Appalachian Mountains to hunt and farm on the frontier lands. The Indians fought against the settlers, believing that previous treaties they had made with the British allowed them the right to stay on these lands. Eventually, the Indians were forced off the lands.

Once the Seven Years' War in Europe was over, Britain, France, and Spain signed another treaty called the Peace of Paris. It spelled out in great detail which islands, nations, and territories throughout the world were to be controlled by each of these countries. This picture shows a celebration in Paris after the Peace of Paris was signed.

Events Leading to the Revolutionary War

Even though Britain now ruled the seas and controlled lands throughout the world, they were in great debt from fighting wars in North America and Europe. To pay their war debts, Britain placed additional taxes on the North American colonists. The colonists thought these taxes were unfair. Even though most colonists at this time did not want to break away from British rule, some started to talk about gaining independence from Great Britain and governing themselves.

In 1775, the North American colonies and Great Britain were still disagreeing about taxes and political rights. From 1775 to 1783, the British and colonial armies fought each other for control of the thirteen North American colonies, a land rich in **economic resources** and opportunities. This conflict was called the Revolutionary War, or the American War of Independence.

After the French and Indian War ended, the British colonies in North America now had to be concerned about fighting between settlers and Indians, as more settlers moved westward.

Glossary

ally   person or group that supports another person or group

artillery   cannons

Bahamas   island colony of Great Britain in the West Indies, southeast of Florida

bayonet   long, pointed knife that attached to the end of a musket

blockade   troops or warships that block enemy troops or supplies from entering or leaving an area

campaign   military mission

carbine   rifle with a short barrel

cartridge   musket ball

cavalry   soldiers who rode horses

colony   territory settled by people from other countries who still had loyalty to those other countries. The word *colonist* is used to describe a person who lives in a colony. The word *colonial* is used to describe things related to a colony.

column   long line of soldiers

commander in chief   highest ranking official in charge of all the military forces

draft   to require men to join the military

economic resource   natural material, such as timber or animal fur, that was in demand and could be sold for a profit

fleet   group of ships

force   group of soldiers

harbor   place along the coastline that provided protection for ships

infantry   foot soldiers

militia   small military unit of ordinary men organized by an individual state. Men who fought in the militia were called *militiamen*.

musket   type of gun with a long barrel

Plains of Abraham   large field outside the walls of the fort in Quebec, Canada

recruit   to get someone to join the military; person who has agreed to sign up for something, usually military service

regiment   group of soldiers

regular   full-time soldier

saber   sword used by the cavalry

sextant   device that used the stars, Moon, and Sun to determine latitude and longitude at sea

skirmish   brief fight, most often between small groups

squadron   part of a larger group of ships

swab   pole with a wad of cloth used to clean the inside of the barrel of a cannon

volley   gunfire from many weapons

West Indies   group of islands between North and South America

Historical Fiction to Read

Keehn, Sally M. *I Am Regina*. New York: Penguin Putnam Books for Young Readers, 1991. Based on a true story about an Indian attack during the time of the French and Indian War where a ten-year-old girl is taken from her home and held by Indians from 1755–1763.

Martin, Les. *Last of the Mohicans: A Step-up Classic*. New York: Random House, 1993. A retelling of James Fenimore Cooper's original story about the friendship between a young white man and his Mohican Indian friends and the story of the conflict between the French and British.

Historical Places to Visit

Fortifications of Quebec National Historic Site
100 Saint-Louis Street
P.O. Box 2474, Main Post Office
Quebec, Quebec G1K 7R3
Canada
Visitor information: (418) 648-7016 or (800) 463-6769
Visit the site of this French and Indian War battle where the British defeated the French in 1759 at one of the last French strongholds in North America. Many bastions, gates, and defense works still stand near the city.

Fort Ticonderoga National Historical Landmark (Fort Carillon)
P.O. Box 390
Ticonderoga, New York 12883
Visitor information: (518) 585-2821
Visit the site where the French defeated a much larger British Army to maintain control of Canada during the French and Indian War. The Garrison Grounds host reenactments, fife and drum performances, and tours in both French and English.

Fort Pitt Museum (Fort Duquesne)
101 Commonwealth Place
Point State Park
Pittsburgh, Pennsylvania 15222
Visitor information: (412) 281-9284
A museum, rebuilt blockhouse, and the outline where the French and British built forts and fought over control of this important strategic position stand on this site where the Allegheny and Monongahela Rivers meet to form the Ohio River.

Index